Grammar

by Dr. Elaine Dion

illustrated by Dianne Ellis

Publisher
Instructional Fair • TS Denison
Grand Rapids, Michigan 49544

About the Author

Dr. Elaine Dion is the coauthor of three books on composition for middle school students. She currently teaches middle school language arts, a position she has held for over 15 years. She has given numerous presentations at state English conferences as well as at NCTE (National Council of Teachers of English) conventions and has published articles in the field of language arts.

Instructional Fair • TS Denison grants the individual purchaser permission to reproduce the student activity materials in this book for noncommercial individual or classroom use only. Reproduction for an entire school or school system is strictly prohibited. No part of this publication may be reproduced for storage in a retrieval system, or transmitted in any form or by any means, electronic, mechanical, recording, or otherwise, without the prior written permission of the publisher. For information regarding permission, write to Instructional Fair • TS Denison, P.O. Box 1650, Grand Rapids, MI 49501.

ISBN: 1-56822-348-X
Grammar
Copyright © 1996 by Instructional Fair • TS Denison
2400 Turner Avenue NW
Grand Rapids, Michigan 49544

All Rights Reserved • Printed in the USA

Table of Contents

Nouns
   Singular and Plural 1
   Common and Proper 2
   Concrete and Abstract 3
   Collective and Compound 4
   Nouns in Action! 5

Pronouns
   Personal 6
   Demonstrative, Interrogative,
      Relative, and Reflexive 7
   Indefinite and Reciprocal 8
   Pronouns in Action! 9

Adjectives
   Descriptive 10
   Positive, Comparative, and
      Superlative Degrees 11
   Limiting 12
   Adjectives in Action! 13

Verbs
   Action and Linking 14
   Verb Phrases 15
   Principal Parts 16
   Verb Tenses 17
   Active and Passive Voice 18
   Verbs in Action! 19

Adverbs
   Adverbs As Modifiers 20
   Positive, Comparative, and
      Superlative Degrees 21
   Adverbs in Action! 22

Prepositions
   Identifying Prepositions 23
   Prepositional Phrases 24
   Adjective and Adverb Phrases 25
   Prepositions in Action! 26

Conjunctions and Interjections
   Coordinating, Correlative, and
      Subordinating 27
   Interjections 28
   Conjunctions and Interjections
      in Action! 29

Sentences
   Kinds of Sentences 30
   Complete Subjects and Predicates 31
   Simple Subjects and Verbs 32
   Compound Subjects and Verbs 33
   Direct Objects and Indirect Objects . . . 34
   Predicate Nouns and Predicate
      Adjectives 35
   Sentences in Action! 36

Clauses
   Independent and Dependent 37
   Simple and Compound Sentences 38
   Complex Sentences 39
   Clauses in Action! 40

Usage
   Subject-Verb Agreement (Nouns) 41
   Subject-Verb Agreement (Pronouns) . . 42
   Subject-Verb Agreement
      (Compound Subjects) 43
   Negatives 44
   Frequently Confused Words 45
   Usage in Action! 46

Capitalization
   I, Days, Months, Holidays 47
   Historic Events, Periods of Time,
      and Documents 48
   Names and Titles of People, Family
      Relationships 49
   First Words 50
   Religious Names, Races,
      Nationalities, Languages 51
   Geographical Names and Structures . . 52
   Titles 53
   Businesses, Organizations,
      Brand Names, Vehicles 54
   Abbreviations, Acronyms, School
      Courses 55
   Capitalization in Action! 56

Answer Key 57

About This Book

Traditional grammar rules often appear unnecessarily rigid and arbitrary. This book attempts to show that grammar plays a more critical role than many people think. Rather than simply following rules to create a "correct" text, writers attempt to make their writing clear as well as interesting to readers. Of course, tradition dictates most grammar rules, but those rules play key roles in helping writers to convey meaning.

Handbooks use varying terms to describe grammatical constructions—often in an attempt to be more descriptive of the function of particular elements. This book uses traditional terms, not because they are more accurate, but because they may be more familiar.

Each unit in this book begins with a rule, followed by a general description. Illustrative examples follow. In many cases, sentence examples and exercises come from the work of published writers, usually from famous writers of classical fiction. These sentences demonstrate grammatical constructions that published writers use. Activities involve practice with these sentences and production of original sentences imitating the published writers' models.

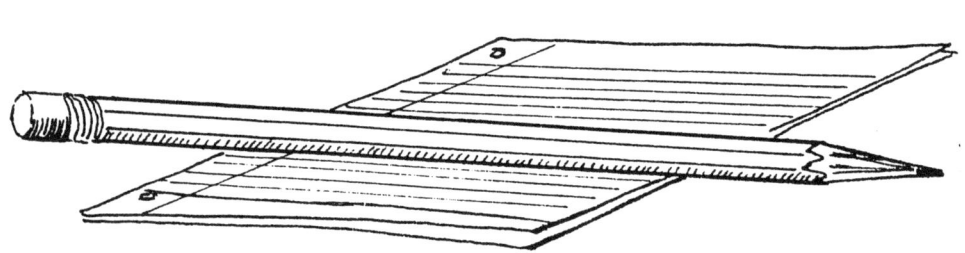

Singular and Plural Nouns

 A noun names a person, place, thing, or idea. A singular noun names one person, place, thing, or idea. A plural noun names more than one person, place, thing, or idea. Plural nouns are often made by adding an -s to the word. If a noun ends in -s, -sh, -ch, -x, or -z, an -es is added. If a noun ends in a consonant followed by -y, the -y is changed to -i and -es is added. For most nouns ending in -f or -fe, an -s is added; however, for some words, the -f or -fe is changed to -v and -es is added.

Singular	Plural	Singular	Plural
horse	horses	church	churches
penny	pennies	day	days
cliff	cliffs	shelf	shelves

Try It!
Following are sentences about the life of Benjamin Franklin. Each sentence contains a singular noun which makes the sentence incorrect. Form the plural of the noun so that the sentence makes sense. Write the plural in the blank provided.

1. Benjamin Franklin became a printer's apprentice to his brother when he was 12 year of age. _____

2. But the brother quarreled, and Benjamin ran away, going first to New York. _____

3. Later, Franklin published a gazette to which he contributed many essay. _____

4. Franklin also conducted many electrical research and continued them to the end of his life. _____

5. In a few years he made many discovery which gave him a reputation throughout Europe. _____

6. His various discoveries affected the life of many. _____

7. Today *Ben Franklin: His Autobiography* ranks as one of the great autobiography of the world. _____

Common and Proper Nouns

 A proper noun names a specific person, place, or thing. Proper nouns are always capitalized. A common noun names a general person, place, thing, or idea. Common nouns are not capitalized unless they begin a sentence.

Proper—Cynthia Voigt   **Common—writer**

Try It!
Write a proper noun for each of the following common nouns.

_____ river   _____ state
_____ book   _____ explorer
_____ building _____ athlete

Try It!
The following sentences about author S. E. Hinton contain both proper and common nouns. Circle each proper noun and underline each common noun.

1. S. E. Hinton has written many novels for young adults.

2. Hinton grew up in Tulsa, Oklahoma.

3. She wrote her first book when she was still in high school in the late 1960s.

4. That novel, *The Outsiders,* was a new type of literature for teenagers because its characters were realistic.

5. The story is about two groups of young people who have problems getting along with each other.

6. Ponyboy is the main character of the story.

7. Ponyboy and Johnny spend time hiding in a church near Windrixville.

8. While at the church the boys read *Gone with the Wind* and recite a poem by Robert Frost called "Nothing Gold Can Stay."

9. Hinton has also written *That Was Then, This Is Now; Tex; Rumble Fish;* and *Taming the Star Runner.*

© Instructional Fair, Inc.   IF2722 Grammar

Concrete and Abstract Nouns

 A concrete noun names a person, place, or thing that can be experienced by one of the senses. An abstract noun names an idea or concept that cannot be experienced by one of the senses.

Concrete—soldier   **Abstract—bravery**

Try It!
Label each of the following nouns, C for concrete and A for abstract.

___ 1. fear   ___ 3. loyalty   ___ 5. football
___ 2. desk   ___ 4. freedom ___ 6. dog

Try It!
In the following sentences about Jack London, write a C in the blank if the italicized noun is concrete and an A in the blank if the italicized noun is abstract.

_____   1. Jack London wrote many wonderful *stories* about the Klondike.

_____   2. He considered good luck, good health, good mental and muscular coordination, and a good brain to be factors in his literary *success*.

_____   3. Because London was born with a strong *body*, his health was good.

_____   4. *Poverty* made London hustle, but good luck prevented poverty from destroying him.

_____   5. As a teenager London was an oyster *pirate*.

_____   6. Many of London's oyster pirate *comrades* were shot, hanged, drowned, killed by disease, or imprisoned, but none of these things happened to London.

_____   7. London felt that for each clever *writer* 20 years ago, 500 clever writers emerged.

_____   8. Excellent writing became swamped in a sea of excellent *writing*.

_____   9. Consequently, *competition* for publishing became fierce.

_____ 10. Reading Herbert Spencer's "Philosophy of Style" taught London how to translate thought, *beauty*, sensation, and emotion into black symbols on white paper.

© Instructional Fair, Inc.   IF2722 Grammar

Collective and Compound Nouns

 A collective noun refers to a group or collection of people or things. Collective nouns are singular. A compound noun consists of two or more words. They may be written as two separate words, as hyphenated words, or as one word.

Collective—team, flock, herd
Compound—middle school, brother-in-law, basketball

Try It!
Each of the following phrases contains either a collective noun or a compound noun. Write the noun and label it **COL** if it is collective and **COM** if it is compound.

                              NOUN   TYPE

1. a flight of stairs   _____   _____

2. a pride of lions   _____   _____

3. a well-thrown football   _____   _____

4. a dilapidated farmhouse   _____   _____

5. a school of fish   _____   _____

Try It!
Each of the following sentences contains either a collective or a compound noun. Circle the noun. In the blank write **COL** if the noun is collective and **COM** if the noun is compound.

_____ 1. Marie Curie and Pierre Curie were a husband and wife team working with radium.

_____ 2. Ernest Hemingway wrote a book about an old fisherman who had not caught a fish for 84 days.

_____ 3. The modern airplane resulted from the imagination and effort of Orville and Wilbur Wright.

_____ 4. Abner Doubleday is often credited with inventing the game of baseball.

_____ 5. Dwight D. Eisenhower was a highly respected general in the army.

Nouns in Action!

To determine whether a word is used as a noun in a sentence, try the following:
1) substitute a personal pronoun for the word in doubt; 2) use the word in doubt after an article, demonstrative adjective, or possessive adjective.

Write a biography of an athlete, explorer, scientist, or politician whom you admire. Your biography should contain at least 12 sentences. Circle all of the nouns. Place each noun under the correct heading. Some nouns may appear in more than one column.

Singular   **Plural**   **Common**   **Proper**

Concrete   **Abstract**   **Collective**   **Compound**

Which type(s) of nouns did you use most frequently? Would your answer change if you had written about a different person? A different topic?

Personal Pronouns

 A personal pronoun takes the place of a noun. Personal pronouns are characterized by their number (singular/plural), case (nominative,

	nominative	possessive	objective
Singular			
first person	I	mine	me
second person	you	yours	you
third person	he, she, it	his, hers, its	him, her, it
Plural			
first person	we	ours	us
second person	you	yours	you
third person	they	theirs	them

Note: *You* may be singular or plural and nominative or objective.

Try It!

Underline the personal pronouns in the following sentences from Chapter 1 of Jack London's *The Call of the Wild*. Then label the case above each using the following abbreviations: **NOM**, **POS**, or **OBJ**.

1. Buck did not read the newspapers, and he did not know that Manuel, one of the gardener's helpers, was an undesirable acquaintance.

2. With the exception of a solitary man, no one saw them arrive at the little flag station known as College Park.

3. When the rope tightened mercilessly around Buck's neck, the surprise was his; Buck struggled in a fury.

4. The express messengers breathed with relief when they bundled him off the train at Seattle.

5. "Well, Buck, my boy," the man in the red sweater went on, "we have had our little ruction. You have learned your place, and I know mine."

Demonstrative, Interrogative, Relative, and Reflexive Pronouns

 Demonstrative pronouns point out, interrogative pronouns ask questions, relative pronouns relate an adjective clause to the noun or pronoun they modify, and reflexive pronouns repeat the subject or refer back to the subject. Singular reflexive pronouns end in -self; plural reflexive pronouns end in -selves.

demonstrative—(singular)—this, that; (plural)—these, those
interrogative—who, whose, whom, which, what
relative—who, whose, whom, which, that
reflexive—(singular)—myself, yourself, himself, itself, herself
(plural)—ourselves, yourselves, themselves

Note: Reflexive pronouns may be called *compound personal pronouns*. *Theirselves* is considered unacceptable in standard usage.

Try It!
The following sentences show the conflict between Buck and Spitz, two dogs in *The Call of the Wild*. Read each sentence. In the first blank write the pronoun. In the second blank state whether it is demonstrative, interrogative, relative, or reflexive. Use the abbreviations **DEM, INT, REL,** and **RFX**.

Pronoun   Type

_____   _____   1. Which is the stronger lead dog, Buck or Spitz?

_____   _____   2. The camp suddenly came alive with four or five score of starving huskies who had scented the camp from some Indian village.

_____   _____   3. As Buck drew himself together to spring after them, out of the trail of his eye, he saw Spitz rush upon him with the evident intention of overthrowing him.

_____   _____   4. He braced himself to the shock of Spitz's charge, then joined the flight out on the lake.

_____   _____   5. It was pride that made Spitz fear Buck as a lead dog.

_____   _____   6. That was Buck's pride, too.

© Instructional Fair, Inc.   IF2722 Grammar

Indefinite and Reciprocal Pronouns

 Indefinite pronouns do not name particular persons, places, or things. They normally have vague antecedents or no antecedents (words to which they refer).

any	anybody	anyone	anything	few
everybody	everyone	everything	nobody	many
no one	nothing	somebody	someone	other
something	each	either	neither	several
none	one	all	both	some

Note: Some indefinite pronouns may also be used as adjectives.

 There are only two reciprocal pronouns. Use each other *when referring to two. Use* one another *when referring to three or more.*

Try It!

In the following sentences, circle all the indefinite and reciprocal pronouns referring to the dogs in *The Call of the Wild*.

1. With Buck as lead dog once more the dogs leaped as one dog in the traces.

2. Dragging sleds over 1,800 miles caused the dogs to suffer, but it was Dave who suffered most of all.

3. Soon Buck was sold to two men who addressed each other as "Hal" and "Charles."

4. Both were out of place, and why they should adventure the North is part of the mystery of things that passes understanding.

5. Three men from a neighboring tent came out and looked on, winking at one another.

6. Hal told his sister that the dogs were lazy, "I tell you, and you've got to whip them to get anything out of them. You ask anyone."

7. Mercedes appealed to everybody and to everything, proceeding to cast out articles that were necessaries.

8. Buck felt that there was no depending on these two men and the woman; they did not know how to do anything.

Pronouns in Action!

Remember that pronouns take the place of nouns when repeating the nouns would become awkward in the sentence. Therefore, try to substitute a noun to determine whether the word is a pronoun.

Try It!
Using the following sentences from Chapter 6 of *The Call of the Wild*, fill in a pronoun that would be appropriate in the sentence. After you are done, compare the pronouns you selected with those that London used.

1. _____ acknowledged Buck a magnificent animal, but twenty
   (indefinite)
   fifty-pound sacks of flour bulked too large in their eyes for _____
   to loosen their pouch strings.   (personal-objective)

2. Thornton did not playfully shake him but _____ whispered in his ear.
                                          (personal-nominative)

3. "As _____ love me Buck," was what he whispered.
      (personal-nominative)

4. Buck threw _____ forward, tightening the traces with a jarring lunge.
              (reflexive)

5. _____ of his feet slipped, and one man groaned aloud.
   (indefinite)

6. As he neared the pile of firewood _____ marked the end
                                      (relative)
   of the hundred yards, a cheer began to grow and grow.

Try It!
Write an animal story of your own or continue the story of Buck. Include at least four different kinds of pronouns.

Descriptive Adjectives

 An adjective describes or modifies a noun or pronoun. One kind of adjective is the descriptive adjective. Descriptive adjectives modify nouns or pronouns by answering the questions what kind? what color? and what size? Proper adjectives are descriptive adjectives. They are derived from proper nouns. They are capitalized.

Descriptive—*loud* music, *red* jersey, *gigantic* apple, *English* tea

Try It!
Read the following sentences about Stephen Crane and his novel, *The Red Badge of Courage*. Circle the descriptive adjective in each sentence. Then write which question each adjective answers in the blank following the sentence.

1. Stephen Crane wrote *The Red Badge of Courage*. _____

2. This famous writer was born in 1871. _____

3. Crane wrote the war novel when he was only 22 years old. _____

4. The story is about Henry Fleming, a young soldier fighting in a war. _____

5. Crane describes realistic scenes of battles with colors. _____

6. Henry wished that he had a wound, a red badge of courage. _____

7. He saw dark waves of men come sweeping out of the woods. _____

8. Behind them blue smoke curled and clouded above the treetops. _____

9. They seemed, for the most part, to be very burly men. _____

10. The youth imagined that he had got into the center of a tremendous quarrel, and he could perceive no way out. _____

11. There was a sinister struggle. _____

12. From the mouths of the men came wild questions, but no one made answers. _____

Positive, Comparative, and Superlative Degrees

 Many adjectives have three degrees: positive *(describes without comparing to anyone or anything else)*, comparative *(compares two people, places, things, or ideas)*, and superlative *(compares three or more people, places, things, or ideas)*. If an adjective consists of one syllable, -er is added to form the comparative degree and -est to form the superlative degree. If the adjective is two or more syllables, more *is placed in front of the positive to form the comparative degree, and* most *is placed in front of the positive to form the superlative degree. If a word consists of more than one syllable and ends in -y, the -y is changed to -i and -er is added to create the comparative degree; -est is added to create the superlative degree.*

	Positive	Comparative	Superlative
one syllable	big	bigger	biggest
two + syllables	creative	more creative	most creative
1 + syllable -y	tiny	tinier	tiniest

Try It!
On the lines write the comparative and superlative degrees of the adjectives listed below.

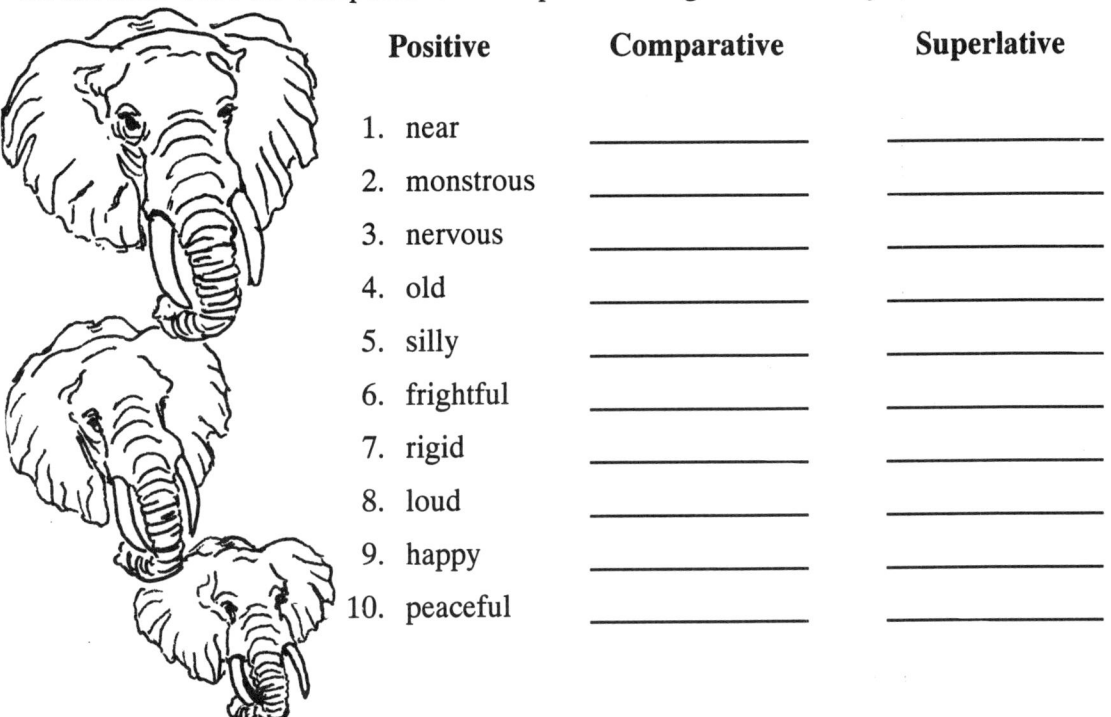

	Positive	Comparative	Superlative
1.	near	_____	_____
2.	monstrous	_____	_____
3.	nervous	_____	_____
4.	old	_____	_____
5.	silly	_____	_____
6.	frightful	_____	_____
7.	rigid	_____	_____
8.	loud	_____	_____
9.	happy	_____	_____
10.	peaceful	_____	_____

© Instructional Fair, Inc. IF2722 Grammar

Limiting Adjectives

 Limiting adjectives do not describe nouns or pronouns. Instead, they show possession, point out, ask questions, limit, or count nouns. They often answer the questions Which one? *and* How many? *and designate particular nouns.*

Possessive (show ownership): my, our, his, her, its, your, their, Mary's
Demonstrative (point out): this, that, these, those
Interrogative (ask questions): which, what, whose
Numeral (numbers modifying nouns): three, third
Articles: a, an, the

Note: *The* is a definite article and designates a particular noun; *a* and *an* are indefinite articles and do not designate a particular noun.

Try It!
Label each limiting adjective *possessive, demonstrative, interrogative, numeral,* or *article*.

1. a _____
2. which _____
3. Bob's _____
4. this _____
5. ten _____
6. those _____
7. eighth _____
8. my _____
9. the _____
10. what _____

Try It!
Circle the limiting adjectives in the sentences below. They depict the scene in *The Red Badge of Courage* when Henry Fleming finds out that his good friend has been shot. There are 12 adjectives.

1. The tall soldier made a little smile. "Hello, Henry," he said.

2. Suddenly, as the two friends marched on, the tall soldier seemed to be overcome by a terror.

3. Jim Conklin was afraid he would fall down and those large artillery wagons would run over him.

4. What advice does the tattered soldier give to Henry?

5. He suggests Henry get Jim out of the road so he won't get run over.

6. Henry's heart was saddened by this terrible sight.

Adjectives in Action!

Descriptive adjectives are often located between a limiting adjective (determiner) and a noun. Their degree (positive, comparative, and superlative) can also be changed. Review both types of adjectives.

Try It!
List each adjective in the proper column. Then label each **limiting adjective** *possessive, demonstrative, interrogative, numeral,* or *article.*

	Descriptive	Limiting
1. sixth	_____	_____ (_____)
2. courageous	_____	_____ (_____)
3. this	_____	_____ (_____)
4. whose	_____	_____ (_____)
5. careful	_____	_____ (_____)
6. softest	_____	_____ (_____)
7. an	_____	_____ (_____)
8. quick	_____	_____ (_____)
9. your	_____	_____ (_____)
10. blue	_____	_____ (_____)

Try It!
While drafting *The Red Badge of Courage,* Stephen Crane replaced proper names of many characters with short, descriptive phrases, such as "the tall soldier" and "the tattered soldier." Crane's frequent use of colors helped produce vivid descriptions, such as "*bronzed* veterans," "*yellow* road," and "*red* sickness of battle." Keeping Crane's use of adjectives in mind, create a short story which contains at least ten adjectives describing one or more characters and at least ten colors. Can you write the story without including proper names? Which types of adjectives are easier to include in your writing?

Action and Linking Verbs

 A verb expresses action or a state of being. Action verbs tell what the subject of the sentence does. The action can be physical or mental. Linking verbs, or verbs of being, join the subject of the sentence to a word that renames or describes the subject. They do not show action. Action verbs can be transitive (verbs which need a direct object to complete their meaning) or intransitive (verbs which do not need a direct object to complete their meaning). Linking verbs are intransitive.

Action verbs: talk, run, speak, think
Linking verbs: am, are, is, was, were, be, been

Try It!
The following sentences are based on Chapter 9 of *Anne of Green Gables* by L. M. Montgomery. Circle the verb in each sentence. If the verb is an action verb, write **ACT** in the blank. If the verb is a linking verb, write **LINK** in the blank.

_____ 1. Anne was out in the orchard.

_____ 2. Mrs. Rachel introduced the real reason for her call.

_____ 3. Anne ran in presently.

_____ 4. She halted confusedly inside the door.

_____ 5. She certainly was an odd-looking little creature in the short tight dress.

_____ 6. Her freckles were more numerous and obtrusive than ever.

_____ 7. "She is terribly skinny and homely, Marilla," Mrs. Rachel said.

_____ 8. Anne stood before Mrs. Rachel, her face scarlet with anger.

_____ 9. "I hate you!"

_____ 10. "How dare you call me skinny and ugly?"

_____ 11. "You are a rude, impolite, unfeeling woman!"

_____ 12. "Anne!" exclaimed Marilla in consternation.

Verb Phrases

 A verb phrase consists of the main verb and one or more auxiliary, or helping, verbs. A verb phrase may contain two, three, or four verbs. Some auxiliary verbs are **am, are, is, was, were, do, did, does, have, has, had, should, would, could, can, may, might, will, be, being, been.**

John *walked* **home.**
John *will walk* **home.**
John *has been walking* **home all week.**
John *should have been running* **for exercise.**

Try It!

Underline the verb phrases in the following sentences based on Chapter 18 of *Anne of Green Gables*. Remember, two, three, or four words should be underlined.

1. One evening Mr. and Mrs. Barry had gone to town.

2. Diana's sister, Minni May, was ill, and Diana implored, "Oh, Anne, do come quick."

3. Minnie May lay on the sofa, feverish and restless, while her hoarse breathing could be heard all over the house.

4. Anne said, "Minni May has croup all right; first we must have lots of hot water."

5. "Mary Joe, you may put some wood in the stove."

6. "It seems to me you might have thought of this before."

7. Mary Joe heated more water than would have been needed for a hospital of croupy babies.

8. Matthew had been obliged to go all the way to Spencervale for a doctor.

9. The doctor remarked, "Anne saved that baby's life, for it would have been too late by the time I got there."

10. He added, "I never saw anything like the eyes of her when she was explaining the case to me."

Principal Parts of Verbs

 Verbs have four principal parts. They are present tense (or infinitive) present participle, past tense, and past participle. Regular verbs have an -ing added to them to form the present participle and have a -d or -ed added to them to form the past tense and past participle. The past and past participle of irregular verbs are formed by changing the spelling in other ways. Occasionally the spelling remains the same.

Present	Present Participle	Past	Past Participle
walk	walking	walked	(have) walked
play	playing	played	(have) played
run	running	ran	(have) run
sing	singing	sang	(have) sung

Try It!
Complete the chart by writing the principal parts of each verb found in *Anne of Green Gables*.

Present	Present Participle	Past	Past Participle
1. go	_____	_____	_____
2. think	_____	_____	_____
3. see	_____	_____	_____
4. suffer	_____	_____	_____
5. remember	_____	_____	_____
6. know	_____	_____	_____
7. approve	_____	_____	_____
8. catch	_____	_____	_____
9. allow	_____	_____	_____
10. look	_____	_____	_____
11. speak	_____	_____	_____
12. want	_____	_____	_____

Verb Tenses

 Verb tenses, which distinguish the "time" of the verb, are created from the principal parts of a verb. Six basic tenses are formed from the principal parts with the aid of helping (auxiliary) verbs.

Present: talk, go   Present Perfect: have talked, has gone
Past: talked, went   Past Perfect: had talked, had gone
Future: will talk, will go   Future Perfect: will have talked, will have gone

Try It!
The following sentences are based on Chapter 23 of *Anne of Green Gables*. Change the italicized verb to the tense given in parentheses. Write the new tense in the blank provided.

_____ 1. Anne *will toss* (past) her red braids.

_____ 2. Anne said, "I *know* (past) a girl in Marysville who could walk the ridgepole of a roof."

_____ 3. "Then I *will dare* (present) you to do it," said Josie defiantly.

_____ 4. "Don't you do it, Anne," entreated Diana. "You *fell* (future) off and be killed."

_____ 5. Anne *will manage* (past) to take several steps before the catastrophe came.

_____ 6. When Diana and the other girls *have rushed* (past perfect) frantically around the house, they found Anne lying all white and limp.

_____ 7. Anne gasped, "Oh, Diana, please *will have found* (present) your father and ask him to take me home."

_____ 8. In his arms he *has carried* (past) Anne, whose head lay limply against his shoulder.

_____ 9. Marilla had a sudden stab of fear and realized what Anne *came* (past perfect) to mean to her.

_____ 10. "Mr. Barry, what *will happen* (present perfect) to her?" she gasped.

Active and Passive Voice

 When a verb is in active voice, the subject of the sentence is doing the action. When a verb is in passive voice, the subject of the sentence is acted upon. Passive voice is created with a form of the verb **be** *and the* **past participle** *of an action verb.*

Active voice: James sang the song.
Passive voice: The song was sung by James.

Try It!
Change the sentences written in active voice to passive voice. Change the sentences written in passive voice to active voice.

1. *Anne of Green Gables* was written by L. M. Montgomery.
   _____

2. Anne Shirley was taken in by Marilla and Matthew Cuthbert.
   _____

3. Gilbert Blythe teased Anne at school.
   _____

4. The exams were not prepared for equally by all students.
   _____

5. Anne and Gilbert both attend Queen's, a well-known school for teachers.
   _____

6. Green Gables was dearly loved by Anne.
   _____

7. Throughout the years many young adults have read this novel.
   _____

Verbs in Action!

If a word can be made into past tense, it is a verb. Many verbs end in *-ed, -en, -ify,* or *-ize.*

Try It!
On another sheet of paper, write a paragraph consisting of at least five sentences. Underline each verb. Label each verb *action* or *linking* and identify its *tense* and its *voice* by placing each verb in the appropriate columns.

	Action	or	Linking
1.	_____		_____
2.	_____		_____
3.	_____		_____
4.	_____		_____
5.	_____		_____

	Present	Past	Future	Present Perfect	Past Perfect	Future Perfect
1.	____	____	____	____	____	____
2.	____	____	____	____	____	____
3.	____	____	____	____	____	____
4.	____	____	____	____	____	____
5.	____	____	____	____	____	____

	Active	or	Passive
1.	_____		_____
2.	_____		_____
3.	_____		_____
4.	_____		_____
5.	_____		_____

Circle the correct label.
1. Anne *has studied.* (present, present perfect)
2. Many subjects *were studied by* Anne. (passive voice, active voice)
3. Anne *is studying.* (present participle, past participle)
4. Anne *will have studied.* (future, future perfect)
5. Anne *must have been studying* very hard. (verb phrase, linking verb)

© Instructional Fair, Inc.

Adverbs As Modifiers

 An adverb modifies a verb, adjective, or other adverb. It answers the questions how? when? where? how often? and to what extent?

Modifying a verb: John reads *quickly*.
Modifying an adjective: John is a *very* tall man.
Modifying an adverb: John reads *too* softly.

Try It!
The following sentences are based on the short story "Rikki-tikki-tavi" by Rudyard Kipling. Each sentence contains an adverb. Underline the adverb. Then circle the word it modifies. In the blank provided, write the question the adverb answers: *how, when, where, how often, to what extent*. **Note:** One sentence contains two adverbs, modifying the same word.

_____ 1. An Englishman and his family had just moved into the bungalow.

_____ 2. His son found a very limp mongoose on the garden path.

_____ 3. They gave Rikki-tikki raw meat, which he liked immensely.

_____ 4. Rikki-tikki's mother had carefully told Rikki what to do if he came across white men.

_____ 5. Then Rikki went out into the garden to see what was to be seen.

_____ 6. He sniffed everywhere until he heard voices.

_____ 7. Nag, the cobra, looked at Rikki-tikki with the wicked snake eyes that never changed their expression.

_____ 8. Nag knew that mongooses in the garden meant death sooner or later for him and his family.

_____ 9. Little did Rikki-tikki know that a snake can turn quickly and bite a mongoose in his eye or lip.

_____ 10. Rikki-tikki saved Teddy's life and was rather amused at all the fuss over him.

Positive, Comparative, and Superlative Degrees

 Like adjectives, adverbs have three degrees: positive, comparative, and superlative. The comparative degree of one-syllable adverbs is made by adding -er to the positive form. The superlative degree is made by adding -est to the positive form. For most adverbs ending in -ly (and, therefore, consisting of two or more syllables), more is added to the positive to create the comparative degree. Most is added to create the superlative degree.

Try It!
Complete the following chart by forming the comparative and superlative degrees of each positive adverb below.

Positive	Comparative	Superlative
1. thoughtfully		
2. late		
3. fast		
4. slowly		
5. sorrowfully		
6. often		
7. easily		
8. quietly		
9. low		
10. far		

Try It!
Circle the correct degree (positive, comparative, or superlative) in each of the sentences below.

1. Sarah read the story (carefully, more carefully, most carefully) than her sister did.
2. She would (soon, sooner, soonest) read than watch television.
3. Jeff was the (athletically, more athletically, most athletically) built player on his team.
4. When Jeff was at bat, he hit the ball very (hard, harder, hardest).
5. Carl read the newspaper article (closely, more closely, most closely) than he needed.

Adverbs in Action!

> When working with adverbs, keep the following in mind:
> 1) Many adverbs end in -ly. However, some -ly words are adjectives as in this sentence: We laughed at the silly clown.
> 2) Adverbs that tell when or how often modify verbs: never, now, then, sometimes.
> 3) Adverbs that tell to what extent usually modify adjectives or other adverbs. They are sometimes called intensifiers because they make other words stronger (or weaker): very, quite, almost, too, rather.
> 4) Negatives are adverbs: not, never, hardly, barely, scarcely, and the contraction n't.

Try It!
On another sheet of paper, create a story about an animal. Or, if you wish, continue the story of Rikki-tikki-tavi. Circle each adverb in your story. Then write the adverb under the appropriate column. Some adverbs may fit in more than one column.

-ly ending	Answers how?	Answers when?	Answers where?

Answers how often?	Answers to what extent?	Negatives

Try It!
How many *-ly* adverbs does your story include? How many negatives does your story contain? Read your story again, this time skipping the circled adverbs. How does the absence of adverbs affect the story? What do adverbs add to your writing?

© Instructional Fair, Inc.

Identifying Prepositions

> ★ *A preposition relates a noun or pronoun (its object) to another word in the sentence. There are one-word, two-word, and three-word prepositions. When a preposition is used without an object, it is an adverb.*

John fell down the stairs. (preposition)
John fell down. (adverb)

Common prepositions are *about, above, across, after, against, among, at, before, beneath, behind, below, beside, between, beyond, by, down, during, except, for, from, in, inside, into, like, near, of, off, on, out, outside, over, through, to, toward, under, until, up, upon, with, within, without, according to, along with, because of, next to, except for, in addition to, in back of, in front of, in spite of, on account of.*

Try It!

Circle all the propositions in the following passage based on Chapter 4 of Frances Hodgson Burnett's novel, *The Secret Garden*. You should have 11 if you find all of them.

"Would you make friends with me?" she said to the robin. And she did not say it in her hard little voice but in a tone so soft and eager and coaxing that Ben Weatherstaff was surprised. "Do you know Dickon?" Mary asked.

She was almost as curious about Dickon as she was about the deserted garden. But just that moment the robin, who had ended his song, gave a little shake of his wings, spread them and flew away.

"He has flown over the wall!" Mary cried out, watching him. "He has flown into the orchard—he has flown across the other wall—into the garden where there is no door!"

"He lives there," said old Ben.

Prepositional Phrases

> *A prepositional phrase includes a preposition, its object, and all the words that modify the object.*

A man was sitting (in an <u>armchair</u>) (before the <u>fire</u>).

Try It!
In the following sentences, based on Chapter 12 of *The Secret Garden,* place parentheses around each prepositional phrase and underline its object.

"I don't know anything about children," said Mr. Craven. "I sent for you today because Mrs. Sowerby said I ought to see you. Her daughter had talked about you."

"She knows all about children," Mary said again in spite of herself.

"She ought to," said Mr. Craven. "I thought her rather bold to stop me on the moor. Now I have seen you I think she said sensible things. Do you want toys, books, dolls?"

"Might I," quavered Mary, "might I have a bit of earth?"

He gazed at her a moment and then passed his hand quickly over his eyes. "Do you—care about gardens so much?" he said slowly.

"I didn't know about them in India," said Mary. "I was always ill and tired and it was too hot. I sometimes made little beds in the sand and stuck flowers in them."

"A bit of earth," he said to himself, and Mary thought that somehow she must have reminded him of something. When he stopped and spoke to her, his dark eyes looked almost soft and kind.

"You can have as much earth as you want," he said.

Adjective and Adverb Prepositional Phrases

 A prepositional phrase may function as an adjective or an adverb. When it acts as an adjective, it modifies a noun or pronoun. When it acts as an adverb, it modifies a verb, an adjective, or another adverb.

Mary found the key *to the garden.* (adjective prepositional phrase)
Mary ran *into the room.* (adverb prepositional phrase)

Try It!
Underline the complete prepositional phrase and draw an arrow to the word it modifies. Then, after the corresponding numbers at the bottom of the page, circle the type of phrase, *adjective* or *adverb*. The sentences are based on Chapter 13 of *The Secret Garden*.

1. She could see a glimmer of light coming beneath the door.

2. Someone was crying in that room, and it was quite a young someone.

3. She walked to the door, and pushed it open, and there she was standing in the room.

4. On the bed was lying a boy, crying fretfully.

5. The boy had a sharp, delicate face the color of ivory.

6. He also had lots of hair which tumbled over his forehead in heavy locks.

1. Adjective or Adverb, Adjective or Adverb
2. Adjective or Adverb
3. Adjective or Adverb, Adjective or Adverb
4. Adjective or Adverb
5. Adjective or Adverb
6. Adjective or Adverb, Adjective or Adverb, Adjective or Adverb

Prepositions in Action!

When prepositional phrases are taken out of the sentence, the sentence usually still makes sense.

Try It!
Complete the following sentences with a preposition so that each sentence makes sense. (These sentences are based on Chapter 20 of *The Secret Garden,* entitled "I Shall Live Forever.") This is the first time Dickon and Mary take Colin outside. After you are done, compare the prepositions you selected with those that Burnett used.

Dickon began to push the wheeled chair slowly and steadily. Mistress Mary walked (1) _____ it and Colin leaned back and lifted his face (2) _____ the sky. The arch (3) _____ it looked very high and the small snowy clouds seemed (4) _____ white birds floating (5) _____ outspread wings (6) _____ its crystal blueness. The wind swept (7) _____ soft big breaths (8) _____ the moor and was strange (9) _____ a wild clear scented sweetness. Colin kept lifting his thin chest to draw it in, and his big eyes looked as if it were they which were listening—listening (10) _____ his ears.

"There are so many sounds (11) _____ singing and humming and calling out," he said. "What is that scent the puffs (12) _____ wind bring?"

They wound in and out (13) _____ the shrubbery and out and round the fountain beds, following their carefully planned route (14) _____ the mere mysterious pleasure (15) _____ it.

Coordinating, Correlative, and Subordinating Conjunctions

 Conjunctions connect words, phrases, and clauses. Coordinating conjunctions connect words, phrases, and clauses of equal value. Correlative conjunctions also connect words, phrases, and clauses of equal value but are found in pairs. Subordinating conjunctions connect clauses of unequal value.

Coordinating: and, but, or, nor, for, so, yet
Correlative: not only . . . but also, neither . . . nor, either . . . or, both . . . and, if . . . then
Subordinating: after, although, because, before, since, unless, until

Try It!

Underline the conjunction in each of the following sentences. Be certain to include both parts of all correlative conjunctions. Then label the type of conjunction in the corresponding blanks using these abbreviations: **CO (coordinating)**, **CR (correlative)**, and **SUB (subordinating)**.

_____ 1. The book was difficult but interesting.

_____ 2. Will you put it on the shelf or in the drawer?

_____ 3. Teresa reads both science fiction and historical fiction.

_____ 4. She read A *Wrinkle in Time* by Madeleine L' Engle, and she enjoyed *No Promises in the Wind* by Irene Hunt as well.

_____ 5. Neither science fiction nor historical fiction interests Jacob.

_____ 6. Although Emillio reads science fiction, he prefers sports novels.

_____ 7. Sports stories move quickly because they contain much action.

_____ 8. In sports stories conflict arises not only because of games but also because of problems with other characters.

_____ 9. Since the ending of the book was confusing, Angelo reread it.

_____ 10. The novel was short yet thought-provoking.

Interjections

 An interjection expresses a feeling. Sometimes an interjection begins a sentence and is followed by a comma. When an interjection begins a sentence and expresses strong feeling, it is followed by an exclamation point. Interjections do not express complete thoughts, but they may appear alone or appear within a sentence. They often make dialogue more realistic. Some commonly used interjections are **wow, well, my, yes,** *and* **no.**

Oh, I forgot my jacket.
Ouch! That hurt.

Try It!

In the blanks provided, write an interjection which completes each sentence. Add a comma or an exclamation point as necessary.

_____ 1. A child ran into the street!

_____ 2. the concert should begin on time.

_____ 3. we'll meet at the mall for lunch.

_____ 4. Was that a spectacular catch!" the coach told his center fielder.

_____ 5. Tyrone hit me with the ball!

_____ 6. we do not have enough money to buy a large pizza.

_____ 7. did you find my watch?

_____ 8. but it may be in a dresser drawer.

_____ 9. A wasp is flying around your head!

_____ 10. my sister certainly bakes wonderful pies.

_____ 11. I cannot finish the job by myself.

_____ 12. I will attend this month's meeting.

Conjunctions and Interjections in Action!

Try It!
The following passage is based on one of Aesop's fables translated by George Fyler Townsend. Write the letter which appears in front of the type of conjunction or interjection that identifies each italicized word or words. If your answer is D or E, supply the necessary punctuation.

    A. Coordinating Conjunction
    B. Correlative Conjunction
    C. Subordinating Conjunction
    D. Interjection followed by a comma
    E. Interjection followed by an exclamation point

A wolf, meeting with a stray lamb, resolved not to lay violent hands on him, *but* (1) to find some plea to justify to the lamb the wolf's right to eat him. He thus addressed him: "Sir, last year you grossly insulted me." "*Indeed*" (2) bleated the lamb in a mournful tone of voice, "*Since* (3) I was not then born, it could not have been I." Then said the wolf, "You feed in my pasture." "*No* (4) good sir," replied the lamb, "I have not yet tasted grass." Again said the wolf, "You drink of my well." "*No*" (5) exclaimed the lamb. "I never yet drank water, *for* (6) as yet my mother's milk is *both* (7) food *and* (7) drink to me." Upon which the wolf seized him *and* (8) ate him up, saying, "*Well* (9) I won't remain supperless, *although* (10) you refute every one of my accusations." The tyrant will always find a reason for his tyranny.

_____ 1.   _____ 6.

_____ 2.   _____ 7.

_____ 3.   _____ 8.

_____ 4.   _____ 9.

_____ 5.   _____ 10.

Kinds of Sentences

 There are four kinds of sentences: declarative, interrogative, imperative, and exclamatory. Declarative sentences state facts and end with periods. Interrogative sentences ask questions and end with question marks. Imperative sentences give commands or make requests and end with periods. Exclamatory sentences express strong feeling and end with exclamation marks.

Declarative: Many refer to baseball as the great American game.
Interrogative: Have you ever seen a professional baseball game?
Imperative: Play ball.
Exclamatory: How lucky he was to hit a grand slam home run!

Try It!
Label each sentence **DEC** for declarative, **INT** for interrogative, **IMP** for imperative, and **EXC** for exclamatory. If the punctuation is incorrect, put the correct punctuation mark in the blank following each sentence.

_____ 1. Is September 9, 1995, a significant date in baseball history. _____

_____ 2. On that date Cal Ripken, Jr., broke Lou Gehrig's record of 2,130 consecutive games played. _____

_____ 3. What an amazing feat that was? _____

_____ 4. Did you see the record-breaking game which was played at Camden Yards in Baltimore, Maryland. _____

_____ 5. Mark that date on your calendar. _____

_____ 6. Wow! Number 8 received a 22-minute, 15-second standing ovation from excited fans! _____

_____ 7. Cal Ripken, Jr., played 2,104 consecutive games at short stop. _____

_____ 8. Look for Cal Ripken, Jr.'s, name in the record books. _____

Complete Subjects and Predicates

 The subject of a sentence tells who or what the sentence is about. The complete subject contains the noun or pronoun that names the topic and all the words that modify it. The predicate of a sentence tells something about the subject. The complete predicate is the verb (or verb phrase) and all the words that modify it.

<u>Four prestigious tournaments</u> (comprise the majors in the sport of golf.)
    (subject)   (predicate)

Try It!
Underline the complete subject and place parentheses around the complete predicate.

1. Those tournaments are the PGA, The Masters, the U.S. Open, and the British Open.
2. Hundreds of golfers try each year to qualify for the professional tour.
3. Qualifying tournaments are held throughout the nation.
4. Several other tour events pay more money in prizes than the majors.
5. The Masters' invitation list always includes the winner of the U.S. Amateur.
6. A professional golfer may win money.
7. An amateur cannot receive money as a prize.
8. One of the better, more recent amateurs is Tiger Woods.
9. This young sensation won the U.S. Amateur in 1994 and 1995.
10. Do you know his real name?
11. His given name is Eldrick Woods.
12. His nickname Tiger has nearly replaced his real name.
13. Tiger's father started him golfing at an extremely young age.

Simple Subjects and Verbs

 A simple subject is a noun or pronoun in the complete subject without its modifiers. It names the person, place, thing, or idea about which something is told. A simple predicate is the verb or verb phrase in the complete predicate without its modifiers. It shows action or a state of being.

Professional <u>football</u> (may attract) more television fans this season.
(Do) <u>you</u> enjoy (watch)ing football on television?

Try It!
Underline the simple subject and place parentheses around the verb (or verb phrase) in the following sentences.

1. A merger agreement between the AFL and the NFL established an interleague championship.

2. Do you know the name of this championship game?

3. The championship was quickly named the Super Bowl.

4. The Green Bay Packers won the first two Super Bowl games in 1967 and 1968.

5. They beat Kansas City and Oakland.

6. The Miami Dolphins were unbeaten in the 1972 season, the first such team in over 30 years to complete a season without a loss.

7. They beat Washington in the Super Bowl in 1973.

8. The next year they became the first team since Green Bay to win two consecutive Super Bowls.

9. January Super Bowls have been the highlight of professional football seasons for over 20 years.

10. Will you watch this year's Super Bowl game?

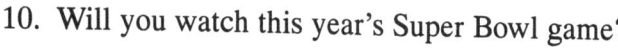

Compound Subjects and Compound Verbs

> ☆ *A compound subject is two or more simple subjects (nouns or pronouns) that have the same verb or verb phrase. A compound verb is two or more verbs (or verb phrases) that have the same subject. Negatives (not, n't) are not part of the verb phrase.*

<u>Volleyball</u> and <u>softball</u> are two popular sports played by many female athletes.
Girls (practice) and (compete) at many levels in both of these sports.

Try It!
Each of the following sentences contains either a compound subject or a compound verb. Underline the compound subjects and place parentheses around the compound verbs.

1. The rules and regulations of volleyball are fairly easy to understand.
2. A point or side-out is awarded for each service.
3. One individual may not touch or be touched by the ball twice in succession.
4. A well-played volleyball game entertains and excites fans.
5. Jenni, Rosa, and Veronica decided to play on their school volleyball team.
6. Rosa will bump, set, and spike today.
7. Jenni and her coach will concentrate on overhand serves.
8. After practice the girls will shower, go home, and rest.
9. During the first game Jenni watched and learned from more experienced players.
10. Both Veronica and Rosa serve and set very well for beginning players.

Direct Objects and Indirect Objects

> ★ *A direct object is a noun in the complete predicate that receives the action of the verb. Direct objects always follow action verbs. An indirect object is a noun in the complete predicate that tells to whom or for whom something is done. Indirect objects follow action verbs and come before direct objects.*

Direct object: The center shot two free throws.
Indirect object: Michael Jordan sent Annie an autographed picture.

Try It!
Underline each direct object and place parentheses around each indirect object.

1. In 1891 an instructor at the YMCA Training School in Springfield, Massachusetts, gave James A. Naismith a job.

2. The instructor wanted a new game for winter recreation.

3. Naismith showed this instructor his new invention.

4. The principles of his game limited body contact in several ways.

5. Instead of tackling, players dribbled the ball.

6. He also used a high horizontal goal.

7. Other rules prohibited body contact without being penalized.

8. Dr. Naismith gave basketball its start with real peach baskets for goals.

9. During the first game, players only scored one goal.

10. Today basketball attracts players and fans of all ages.

Predicate Nouns and Predicate Adjectives

> A predicate noun is a noun or pronoun in the complete predicate that renames the subject. Predicate nouns always follow linking verbs. A predicate adjective is an adjective in the complete predicate that describes the subject. Predicate adjectives also always follow linking verbs.

Predicate noun: Martina Navratilova is an excellent tennis player.
Predicate adjective: Even as a young player she was extremely talented.

Try It!
Underline each predicate noun and place parentheses around each predicate adjective.

1. In the tennis world Wimbledon is one of the most important tournaments.
2. Wimbledon's Centre Court, with its Royal Box, is a focal point of competition in tennis.
3. Arthur Ashe was the first black male to reach the finals at Wimbledon.
4. Ashe was very popular with other professional tennis players because of his dignity both on and off the court.
5. The U.S. Open tournament is the American equivalent of The Championships at Wimbledon.
6. Going late into the night, Manuel Orantes' semifinal match in the 1975 Open was exhausting.
7. Many fans thought Orantes was tired.
8. However, his returns were accurate.
9. Connors was the more aggressive of the two players.
10. Orantes won the match, and Connors was the victim of an upset.

Sentences in Action!

Writers must know several things before writing a sports article or column. First, they must possess knowledge of the game, including its rules, jargon (specialized terms), and players. Second, they must use verbs which portray vivid action and the excitement of the game or match.

Try It!

Select a sport of your own choice from the following: hockey, basketball, baseball, football, boxing, golf, tennis, and volleyball. On another sheet of paper, write about a particular game or match that you have watched. Capture the action and the excitement of the game with vivid subjects and verbs.

After you complete your writing, do the following:

1. Label each sentence according to its type: declarative, interrogative, imperative, or exclamatory.

2. Label each subject, verb, direct object, indirect object, predicate noun, and predicate adjective.

3. Answer the following questions:

    How many of your sentences are declarative? _____

    How many of your sentences are interrogative? _____

    How many of your sentences are imperative? _____

    How many of your sentences are exclamatory? _____

    How many of your sentences contain a direct object? _____

    How many of your sentences contain an indirect object and a direct object? _____

    How many of your sentences contain a predicate noun? _____

    How many of your sentences contain a predicate adjective? _____

4. Find a sports article. Follow the same labeling procedure. Compare your sentences to those of a professional sports writer. Are they similar?

Independent and Dependent Clauses

> A **clause** *is a group of words that contains a subject and a verb. An* **independent clause** *(also called a* **main clause***) can stand by itself as a sentence. A* **dependent clause** *(also called a* **subordinate clause***) does not express a complete thought and, therefore, cannot stand by itself as a sentence.*

In the following example, the independent clause is underlined, and the dependent clause is not.
<u>Each girl thought of Father far away</u> where the fighting was.

Try It!
The following sentences are based on Chapter 1, "Playing Pilgrims," of Louisa May Alcott's *Little Women*. Circle IC if the clause is independent. Circle DC if the clause is dependent. Since all begin with capital letters and end with periods, careful reading is a must.

- IC DC 1. Because it is going to be a hard winter for everyone.
- IC DC 2. She thinks we ought not to spend money for pleasure.
- IC DC 3. When our men are suffering in the army.
- IC DC 4. Meg shook her head.
- IC DC 5. As she thought regretfully of all the pretty things she wanted.

Try It!
Following are additional sentences based on Chapter 1 of *Little Women*. Underline each independent clause and place parentheses around each dependent clause.

1. The four sisters sat knitting away in the twilight while the December snow fell quietly.
2. Beth looked at her rough hands with a sigh that anyone could hear.
3. Although we have to work, we make fun for ourselves.
4. I like your nice manners and refined ways of speaking when you don't try to be elegant.
5. If Jo is a tomboy, what am I please?

© Instructional Fair, Inc.

IF2722 Grammar

Simple and Compound Sentences

☆ *A simple sentence contains one independent clause and, therefore, expresses one complete thought. It may have a simple subject or a compound subject and a simple verb or a compound verb. However, a simple sentence cannot contain a dependent clause.*

☆ *A compound sentence consists of two or more simple sentences joined together by a comma and a coordinating conjunction or by a semicolon.*

Simple Sentence: Meg looked over her dress and sang.
Compound Sentence: Jo finished her story, and she played a game of romps with Scrabble.

Try It!

The following sentences are based on Chapter 3 of *Little Women*. Label each simple sentence **SIMP** and each compound sentence **COMP** in the blanks provided. If the sentence is compound, circle the comma and coordinating conjunction or the semicolon.

_____ 1. At one time a strong smell of burnt hair pervaded the house.

_____ 2. Meg wanted a few curls about her face, and Jo undertook to pinch the papered locks with a pair of hot tongs.

_____ 3. Jo took off the papers, but no cloud of ringlets appeared.

_____ 4. The hair came with the papers, and the horrified hairdresser laid a row of little scorched bundles on the bureau before her victim.

_____ 5. Meg looked with despair at the uneven frizzle on her forehead.

_____ 6. "You shouldn't have asked me to do it; I always spoil everything."

_____ 7. "I'm so sorry."

_____ 8. "The tongs were too hot, and so I've made a mess."

_____ 9. Jo groaned, regarding the little black pancakes with tears of regret.

_____ 10. "Tie your ribbon so the ends come on your forehead a bit, and it will look like the latest fashion."

Complex Sentences

> ⭐ A complex sentence contains one independent clause and one or more dependent clauses. Relative pronouns introduce dependent clauses that function as adjectives: *who, whose, whom, which,* and *that.* Subordinate conjunctions introduce dependent clauses that function as adverbs. Some commonly used subordinate conjunctions are *after, although, because, if, since, unless, until, when,* and *while.*

Adjective Clause: Amy March, <u>who got twenty-four delicious limes</u>, was going to treat her friends.

Adverb Clause: <u>Because Amy had not forgotten Jenny Snow's cutting remarks</u>, she refused to give her a lime.

Try It!
Underline each dependent clause in the following sentences based on Chapter 7 of *Little Women*. If the dependent clause is used as an adjective, write ADJ in the blank. If the dependent clause is used as an adverb, write ADV in the blank.

_____ 1. Jenny informed Mr. Davis it was Amy March who had pickled limes in her desk.

_____ 2. Mr. Davis had solemnly vowed to publicly punish the first person who was found breaking the law.

_____ 3. Mr. Davis rapped on his desk with an energy which made Jenny skip to her seat with unusual rapidity.

_____ 4. A secret fear oppressed Amy because the limes weighed upon her conscience.

_____ 5. Since Amy had many, she shook out half a dozen.

_____ 6. She felt Mr. Davis would relent when the perfume met his nose.

_____ 7. Because they were so disgusting, the teacher made Amy throw the limes out of the window.

_____ 8. There was a simultaneous sigh, which created quite a little gust, and the treat was ravished from their longing lips.

_____ 9. On the street little Irish children, who were sworn foes of the girls, enjoyed the limes.

_____ 10. After Amy disposed of the treat, Mr. Davis made her stand on the platform until recess.

Clauses in Action!

Try It!
Change the clauses in the following short paragraphs to give them more variety. The clauses are based on Chapter 28 of *Little Women*.

1. Jo's face was very sober. Jo's eyes twinkled. (Change to a compound sentence using , *but* to join.)

2. "Shut your eyes," she said invitingly. "Hold out your arms," she said invitingly. (Change the quotation to a simple sentence with a compound verb.)

3. Laurie backed into a corner. He put his hands behind him with a gesture. (Change to a simple sentence with a compound predicate.)

4. Laurie heroically shut his eyes. Something was put into his arms. (Change to a complex sentence. Begin the dependent clause with *while*.)

5. Jo laughed at Laurie. Amy laughed at Laurie. John laughed at Laurie. (Change to a simple sentence with a compound subject.)

6. John rescued his babies. Laurie laughed saying, "Twins, by Jupiter!" (Change to a complex sentence. Begin the dependent clause with *when*.)

Subject-Verb Agreement (Nouns)

> ☆ *The subject and verb of a sentence must agree in number. Singular subjects take singular verbs, and plural subjects take plural verbs. Most verbs are made singular by adding -s or -es to them. Is, was, has, and does are singular and are used with singular subjects. Are, were, have, and do are plural and are used with plural subjects. Note: The subject, not the object of a preposition, must agree with the verb.*

The chickadee is the state bird of Massachusetts.
Cranberries grow in the soggy soil of bogs in this state.
The state bird of Massachusetts is the chickadee.

Try It!

Underline the subject of each sentence. Then circle the verb which makes each sentence grammatically correct.

1. The Appalachian Trail (wind, winds) from Maine to Georgia.

2. It (run, runs) through western Massachusetts.

3. The Berkshire Hills also (are, is) found in western Massachusetts.

4. Many lovers of music (attend, attends) the Berkshire Festival at Tanglewood.

5. Boston (lie, lies) on the eastern coast of Massachusetts.

6. In Boston red lines on the sidewalks (mark, marks) the Freedom Trail.

7. Tourists (walk, walks) this trail to see historic sites such as Faneuil Hall and the Old North Church.

8. A bronze statue of Paul Revere on horseback (stand, stands) behind Boston's Old North Church.

9. Three professional sports' teams (make, makes) their home in Boston, the Celtics, the Red Sox, and the Bruins.

10. Harvard in Cambridge, Massachusetts, (is, are) the oldest college in the United States.

Subject-Verb Agreement (Pronouns)

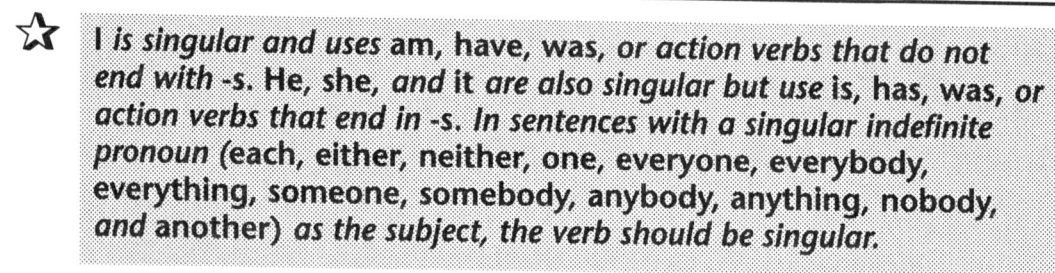

☆ *I is singular and uses* am, have, was, *or action verbs that do not end with -s.* He, she, *and* it *are also singular but use* is, has, was, *or action verbs that end in -s. In sentences with a singular indefinite pronoun (*each, either, neither, one, everyone, everybody, everything, someone, somebody, anybody, anything, nobody, *and* another*) as the subject, the verb should be singular.*

☆ *In sentences with a plural indefinite pronoun (*both, many, few, *and* several*) as the subject, the verb should be plural.*

☆ *Indefinite pronouns (*all, any, most, none, *and* some*) may be either singular or plural. When these indefinite pronouns are subjects, the verb should agree with the objects of the prepositions.*

Everybody cheers loudly at games.
Few score as many hockey goals as Wayne Gretsky.
Some of the mail was late. Some of the letters were missing.

Try It!

Underline the subject (which is an indefinite pronoun) of each sentence. Then circle the verb which makes the sentence grammatically correct.

1. Everybody (like, likes) to visit new places.
2. Many (travel, travels) to warm-weather climates during the winter months.
3. Neither of the bus drivers (know, knows) the best route from Houston, Texas, to Key West, Florida.
4. Some of the tourists (want, wants) to do additional sightseeing in the Keys.
5. Several of the sites (was, were) breath-taking.
6. (Have, Has) any of these travelers been to the Everglades, west of Miami?
7. Everyone (agree, agrees) that Disney World continues to make tourism a major activity in Florida.
8. Many (want, wants) to buy sponges at Tarpon Springs, the nation's leading producer of sponges.
9. Most of the tourists (enjoy, enjoys) the Everglades.
10. All of the trip to Florida (was, were) enjoyable.

Subject-Verb Agreement (Compound Subjects)

> ★ *In sentences with compound subjects joined by and, the verb should be plural. In sentences with a compound subject joined by or or nor, the verb should agree with the subject nearer to it.*

Sherry and Sarah enjoy traveling to new places.
Sherry or her brothers travel at least once a year.
Her brothers or Sherry travels at least once a year.

Try It!
If the compound subject needs a singular verb to make it grammatically correct, circle *is*. If the compound subject needs a plural verb to make it grammatically correct, circle *are*.

1. Mountains and the forest — is   are
2. The Grand Coulee or other Columbia dams — is   are
3. The Olympic Mountains and the Cascades — is   are
4. Seattle or Spokane — is   are
5. Apples or salmon — is   are
6. The capital or other Puget Sound cities — is   are
7. Ships and tankers — is   are
8. Mount Saint Helens or Mount Baker — is   are
9. Lumber, wood products, and paper products — is   are
10. Colville Indian Reservation or Yakima Indian Reservation — is   are

Try It!
Underline the verb which makes the sentence grammatically correct.

1. Carlos, Ricardo, and James (like, likes) the Pacific Northwest.
2. The Butchart Gardens in Victoria and Stanley Park in Vancouver (is, are) beautiful places that the young men plan to visit.
3. Carlos or Ricardo (know, knows) the ferry ride from Victoria to Anacortes, Washington, will show them the beauty of the San Juan Islands.
4. Ricardo and James (want, wants) to see the Grand Coulee Dam on the Columbia River.
5. The rich soil and mild climate (help, helps) trees, moss, ferns, and vines to grow.

© Instructional Fair, Inc.   IF2722 Grammar

Negatives

> ☆ *Standard usage avoids double negatives in the same sentence. Many negatives begin with the letter -n: no, none, not (n't), nothing, never, neither, no one, nobody, and nowhere. A few words may be considered "mildly" negative and do not begin with -n: hardly, barely, and scarcely.*

> ☆ *When no is followed by a comma, it is acceptable to use another negative after the comma: No, Karen hasn't forgotten her promise.*

    poor: John did*n't* do *nothing* wrong.
  better: John did*n't* do *anything* wrong.
           John *did nothing* wrong.

    poor: John could *not barely* see the road.
  better: John could *not* see the road.
           John *could barely* see the road.

Try It!

Rewrite each of the following sentences eliminating the double negatives. Note: There may be more than one way to eliminate the double negative correctly.

1. Richard can't hardly wait for the next tour.

2. He hadn't gone nowhere since the trip to the Southwest.

3. Jacob has not found no postcards.

4. No, Susan did not see nobody she knew while visiting in Duluth, Minnesota.

5. During the 1930s nobody did nothing to prevent damage caused by strip mining in the Southwest.

Frequently Confused Words

> ☆ *The following words are frequently confused in sentences.*
>
> *beside/besides:* Beside *means "by the side of";* besides *means "in addition to." Jeff sat* beside *Sharon at the meeting.* Besides *hamburgers, chicken was served.*
>
> *fewer/less:* Fewer *refers to the number of separate items;* less *refers to quantity (items than cannot be counted). I received* fewer *letters this week than last week. I received* less *mail this year than last year.*
>
> *good/well:* Good *is an adjective meaning "what kind";* well *is an adverb meaning "how something is done." Susan is a* good *pianist. Susan plays the piano* well.
>
> *than/then:* Than *is a conjunction used after the comparative degree of an adjective;* then *is an adverb meaning "next." Todd is taller* than *his brother. First it rained;* then *it snowed.*

Try It!
Circle the word that makes the sentence grammatically correct.

1. (Fewer, Less) people will vacation in Montana than in Arizona this year.
2. (Beside, Besides) the Grand Canyon, the group also went to Pike's Peak.
3. We experienced (fewer, less) traffic around Atlanta, Georgia, than we expected.
4. John had a (good, well) time at the CNN building in Atlanta.
5. Troy wanted to ski in Vail, Colorado, because his brother taught him how to ski (good, well).
6. Las Vegas boasts over 88,000 motel rooms; often one motel is right (beside, besides) another.
7. They golfed at Pebble Beach; (then, than) they ate dinner in Monterey.
8. Jerry's score was higher (then, than) Joe's score.
9. Joe was a (good, well) loser and bought dinner.
10. The group played (fewer, less) matches on this vacation.

Usage in Action!

Tourism is vital to the economy in some areas of the United States. In fact, many people make their living by catering to travelers. Vying for dollars that tourists will spend becomes serious business. Consequently, advertisements must attract potential customers—and language, the use of the right words, helps to promote this attraction.

Try It!

Create a travel brochure about a place that you have visited or a place that you would like to visit. (You may wish to study several brochures at a local travel agency.) Remember, in addition to pictures, appropriate language sells! Use specific nouns, vivid adjectives, and action verbs. Pay careful attention to subject/verb agreement, double negatives, and frequently confused words. Begin a first draft of what you would like to say in your travel brochure here.

Capitalization
(I, Days, Months, Holidays)

☆ *Always capitalize the pronoun I regardless of where it appears in a sentence.*

☆ *Capitalize the names of the days of the week, months, and holidays. Do not capitalize the names of seasons.*

Mary and I read *A Christmas Carol.*
Monday, April, Thanksgiving, spring.

Try It!
Only one sentence in each group is capitalized correctly. Write the letter of that sentence in the blank provided.

_____ 1. A. Charles Dickens wrote *A Christmas Carol* between October and november of 1843.

_____ B. Charles Dickens wrote *A Christmas Carol* between October and November of 1843.

_____ 2. A. The first edition of this book was ready by December 17 of that same Winter.

_____ B. The first edition of this book was ready by December 17 of that same winter.

_____ C. The first edition of this book was ready by december 17 of that same winter.

_____ 3. A. Early in the story Scrooge says, "Bah! Humbug!" in response to his nephew's wishes for a joyful christmas.

_____ B. Early in the story Scrooge says, "Bah! Humbug!" in response to his nephew's wishes for a joyful Christmas.

_____ 4. A. "I wish to be left alone," said Scrooge. "I don't make merry myself at Christmas, and I can't afford to make idle people merry."

_____ B. "I wish to be left alone," said Scrooge. "I don't make merry myself at Christmas, and i can't afford to make idle people merry."

_____ 5. A. Scrooge thought the Holiday was a poor excuse for picking a man's pocket every twenty-fifth of december.

_____ B. Scrooge thought the holiday was a poor excuse for picking a man's pocket every twenty-fifth of December.

© Instructional Fair, Inc.   IF2722 Grammar

Capitalization (Historic Events, Periods of Time, and Documents)

> ★ Capitalize all important words in the names of historical events, periods of time, and titles of documents. Do not capitalize articles, conjunctions, or short prepositions unless they are the first word of the name or title.

World War II, Boston Tea Party
Period of Enlightenment, Reformation
Magna Carta, the Monroe Doctrine

Try It!
Capitalize the historic events, periods of time, and documents by circling each letter that needs a capital.

1. the mayflower compact
2. articles of confederation
3. french and indian war
4. the gettysburg address
5. the declaration of independence
6. great depression
7. valentine's day massacre
8. missouri compromise
9. the emancipation proclamation
10. renaissance

Try It!
If a word is capitalized that should not be, draw a diagonal (/) through the capitalized letter. If a word is not capitalized and should be, circle the letter that needs to be capitalized.

1. During the middle ages the Middle Class grew in number and importance.
2. Artists and Writers created new styles and techniques during the renaissance.
3. Freedom of press and of speech are guaranteed in the bill of Rights.
4. The battle of gettysburg was a significant Battle in the civil War.
5. The Louisiana purchase doubled the size of the United States.
6. Many people moved to cities to work in Industry as a result of the industrial revolution.
7. The Stock Market Crash of 1929 was only one cause of the great depression.
8. On January 16, 1991, president bush announced that Operation desert shield had become Operation desert storm.

Capitalization (Names and Titles of People, Family Relationships)

☆ *Capitalize the names of people and initials or abbreviations that take the place of the names.*

☆ *Capitalize titles (and abbreviations of those titles) used with names of people. Do not capitalize a title when the title alone is used.*

☆ *Capitalize the titles of relatives when they are used in place of a person's name.*

Horatio Alger, J. R. R. Tolkien

General Eisenhower, Dr. Holmes; I went to the doctor yesterday.

Give the car keys to Father. I gave the car keys to my father.

Try It!
Circle Y if the name/title is capitalized correctly. Circle N if it is not.

Y N 1. rabbi Gold   Y N 5. Mr. Paul Lowman
Y N 2. Dr. Elizabeth Shumate   Y N 6. the general
Y N 3. governor Thompson   Y N 7. my Cousin
Y N 4. Cousin Rachel   Y N 8. prince Charles

Try It!
Circle the first letter of each word that should be capitalized. If a word is capitalized and should not be, draw a diagonal (/) through the incorrectly capitalized letter.

1. *The wizard of Oz* was written by L. Frank Baum in 1900.

2. Dorothy lived in the midst of the great Kansas prairies with uncle Henry, who was a farmer, and aunt Em, who was the farmer's wife.

3. Neither Dorothy's Aunt nor her Uncle smiled; they were the same gray which was seen everywhere.

4. Tom Sawyer is another character who lived with his Aunt, aunt Polly.

5. Samuel l. clemens often wrote under his pen name, mark twain.

6. In *The Secret Garden,* Mary Lennox lives in her Uncle's house, and in *Heidi* the main character lives with grandfather.

Capitalization (First Words)

☆ *Capitalize the first word of every sentence.*

☆ *Capitalize the first word in a direct quotation.*

☆ *Capitalize the first word of each line of a traditional poem. (Note: often modern poets do not follow this rule.)*

My sister reads novels and poetry.
Miguel asked, "Have you read *Ragged Dick* yet?"
Now Sam McGee was from Tennessee, where the cotton blooms and blows.

Try It!
Circle the first letter of each word that requires capitalization.
1. lewis Carroll created his own words to write the poem "Jabberwocky."
2. that poem appears in the story *Alice's Adventures in Wonderland*.
3. One of the lines in this poem reads: "and burbled as it came!"
4. The last stanza of the poem begins with the following two lines: " 'twas brillig, and the slithy toves/did gyre and gimble in the wabe."
5. Susan asked, "have you read Carroll's book?"
6. "yes, and I enjoyed the poem although I didn't understand every word," Pat answered.
7. another poet, William Service, wrote many poems about the Yukon.
8. "The Cremation of Sam McGee" contains the following line used in the refrain of the poem: "there are strange things done in the midnight sun."
9. "service's poem would make an interesting choral reading," Milo remarked.
10. he added, "i liked how Sam McGee played a trick on his partner to get warm."

Capitalization (Religious Names, Races, Nationalities, and Languages)

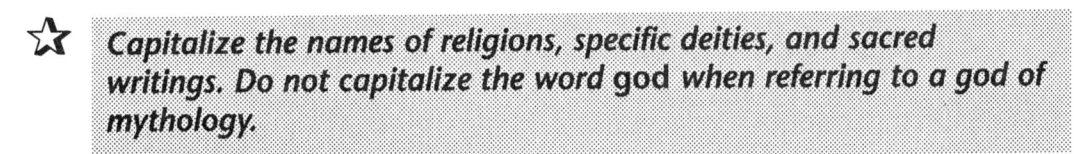

☆ *Capitalize the names of religions, specific deities, and sacred writings. Do not capitalize the word god when referring to a god of mythology.*

☆ *Capitalize the names of races.*

☆ *Capitalize the names of nationalities and languages.*

Baptist religion, Hindu faith, the Almighty, a Greek god Zeus
Native American, Caucasian
Italian, French

Try It!
Circle Y if the phrase is capitalized correctly. Circle N if it is not.

Y N 1. a Portuguese explorer	Y N 6. the Protestant faith
Y N 2. the Bible	Y N 7. speak spanish
Y N 3. the Book of genesis	Y N 8. the old testament
Y N 4. a french citizen	Y N 9. pray to god
Y N 5. Poseidon, god of the sea	Y N 10. the Book of Mormon

Try It!
Circle the first letter of each word that should be capitalized.

1. Matthew, Mark, luke, and john are the first four books of the new testament.
2. The pope is a respected leader in the catholic religion.
3. Debbie speaks japanese as well as english.
4. The chinese language is spoken by millions of people.
5. The congregation prayed to the almighty at the beginning and the end of the service.

Capitalization (Geographical Names and Structures)

☆ *Capitalize important words in geographical names.*

☆ *Capitalize names of sections of a country but not directions.*

☆ *Capitalize important words in the names of buildings, bridges, and other structures.*

Pacific Ocean, Bay of Good Hope
We traveled west. John lives in the Southwest.
Empire State Building, Statue of Liberty, Washington Monument

Try It!
Circle the first letter of each word that should be capitalized. If a word is capitalized that should not be, draw a diagonal (/) through the incorrectly capitalized letter.

1. We walked East three blocks to the white house.

2. Many who visit chicago ride to the top of sears tower to view the City.

3. We drove along lake shore drive and then shopped at water tower place on Michigan avenue.

4. Many people from the north retire in the southeast or the Southwest.

5. In 1929, Gutzon Borglum began to carve mount rushmore out of the granite in the black Hills Of south Dakota.

6. The climate in Central america is more temperate than the climate in Northern texas.

7. Lake Of The Woods lies Northwest of International Falls, Minnesota.

8. The leaning tower of Pisa in italy and the Eiffel tower in France are two famous Structures in Europe.

9. Very few plants grow in the cinders of crater Of the Moon National monument in southeastern idaho.

10. lake Superior, lake Michigan, lake Huron, lake erie, and lake ontario, the five Great lakes, hold approximately one fourth of all the fresh water in the world.

© Instructional Fair, Inc.

IF2722 Grammar

Capitalization (Titles)

> ★ *Capitalize the first word, last word, and all important words in titles. Note: Do not capitalize the word* the *when it appears before titles of newspapers and magazines.*

Book: *The Call of the Wild*
Magazine: *Car and Driver*
Newspaper: the *Des Moines Register*
Poem: "The Cremation of Sam McGee"
Short Story: "The Ransom of Red Chief"
Movie: *Jaws II*
Play: *Our Town*

Try It!
Circle the first letter of each word that should be capitalized.

1. Joseph Pulitzer acquired the *st. Louis dispatch*, the *st. Louis post*, the *new york world*, and the *evening world* among other newspapers.

2. In the late 1800s Horatio Alger became wealthy with his more than 100 rags-to-riches novels, *struggling upward* and *ragged Dick* among the most successful.

3. John Steinbeck wrote newspaper articles for the *san Francisco news* on migrant workers and wrote a magazine story about flood victims for *life* magazine.

4. The information from these articles later appeared in Steinbeck's *the grapes of wrath*.

5. On May 8, 1851, the Hannibal *western union* described a man and a wife with four or five children living in a hogshed.

6. Mark Twain quite possibly molded that excerpt into his book, *the adventures of huckleberry finn*.

7. Ray Bradbury used Sara Teasdale's poem entitled "There will come soft Rains" for the theme and plot of a story to which he gave the same title.

8. English playwright William Shakespeare wrote over 100 sonnets as well as famous plays, such as *romeo and juliet* and *the taming of the shrew*.

9. Likewise, Edgar Allan Poe wrote the famous poems "the raven" and "annabel lee" as well as chilling stories, such as "the tell-tale heart."

10. Jack London first published "to build a fire" in *youth's companion*.

Capitalization (Businesses, Organizations, Brand Names, Vehicles)

★ *Capitalize all important words in the names of businesses and organizations.*

★ *Capitalize a brand name but not the common noun that follows the brand name.*

★ *Capitalize the names of ships, trains, aircraft, and brand names of automobiles.*

New Mexico Military Institute, Bank of Chicago
Campbell's soup
USS *Missouri*, *Orient Express*, *Concorde*, **Ford convertible**

Try It!
Write the letter of the sentence that is capitalized correctly in the blank provided.

_____ 1. A. The *Titanic* hit an iceberg and sunk on its maiden voyage.
            B. The *titanic* hit an iceberg and sunk on its Maiden Voyage.

_____ 2. A. For many years the beautiful ship, the *Queen Mary*, and the *Spruce Goose*, a plane owned by Howard Hughes, could be seen in Long Beach, California.
            B. For many years the beautiful ship, the *queen Mary*, and the *spruce Goose*, a plane owned by Howard Hughes, could be seen in Long Beach, California.

_____ 3. A. Nike athletic shoes and Guess jeans have been popular casual wear with teenagers and young adults.
            B. Nike Athletic Shoes and Guess Jeans have been popular casual wear with teenagers and young adults.

_____ 4. A. The Mustang convertible looks extremely different from the Model T.
            B. The Mustang Convertible looks extremely different from the model t.

Capitalization (Abbreviations, Acronyms, School Courses)

☆ *Capitalize the two-letter postal abbreviations for states when using addresses that include the ZIP code.*

☆ *Capitalize the abbreviations A.M., P.M., B.C., and A.D. Note that B.C. follows the date and that A.D. precedes the date.*

☆ *Capitalize acronyms (an acronym is composed of the first letters of each word in a phrase).*

☆ *Capitalize the name of a school subject if it is a language or if it is followed by a course number.*

Oro Valley, AZ 85737   **YMCA (Young Men's Christian Association)**
A.M., P.M., B.C., and A.D.   **Spanish, American History 101, algebra**

Try It!

Rewrite the following phrases capitalizing all letters that should be capitalized.

1. left at 7:30 p.m. _____
2. assignment for spanish II _____
3. in 1300 b.c. _____
4. took archery 110 _____
5. unicef collection _____
6. took place in a.d. 603 _____
7. mail to Beverly Hills, Ca 90210 _____
8. swimming at the ymca _____
9. send via the Fax machine _____
10. ends at 10:13 a.m. _____
11. loaded dos on the computer _____
12. changed from 1000 b.c. to a.d. 1000 _____
13. member of nato _____
14. contributed to the naacp _____

Capitalization in Action!

Try It!
Write an original sentence including the specific elements listed below. Capitalize each sentence correctly.

1. a monument east of the Mississippi River

   _____

2. a body of water larger than a pond

   _____

3. a title of a book or poem written after 1910

   _____

4. the name and title of a person with whom you are familiar

   _____

5. a city and state which you have never visited

   _____

6. two school subjects

   _____

7. a time after noon and the name of a building

   _____

8. a historical event before the Civil War

   _____

9. the title of a book and the title of a poem

   _____

10. the title of a movie and a brand name

    _____

Answer Key

Singular and Plural Nouns   page 1
1. years
2. brothers
3. essays
4. researches
5. discoveries
6. lives
7. autobiographies

Common and Proper Nouns   page 2
1. S. E. Hinton—proper; novels, adults—common
2. Hinton, Tulsa, Oklahoma—proper
3. book, high school, 1960s—common
4. *The Outsiders*—proper; novel, type, literature, teenagers, characters—common
5. story, groups, people, problems—common
6. Ponyboy—proper; character, story—common
7. Ponyboy, Johnny, Windrixville—proper; time, church—common
8. *Gone with the Wind*, Robert Frost, "Nothing Gold Can Stay"—proper; church, boys, poem—common
9. Hinton, *That Was Then, This Is Now, Tex, Rumble Fish, Taming the Star Runner*—proper

Concrete and Abstract Nouns   page 3
1. A
2. C
3. A
4. A
5. C
6. C

1. C
2. A
3. C
4. A
5. C
6. C
7. C
8. C
9. A
10. A

Collective and Compound Nouns   page 4
1. flight — COL
2. pride — COL
3. football — COM
4. farmhouse — COM
5. school — COL

1. team — COL
2. fisherman — COM
3. airplane — COM
4. baseball — COM
5. army — COL

Nouns in Action!   page 5
Answers will vary.

Personal Pronouns   page 6
1. he — NOM
2. them — OBJ
3. his — POS
4. they — NOM
   him — OBJ
5. we — NOM
   You — NOM
   I — NOM
   mine — POS

Demonstrative, Interrogative, Relative, and Reflexive Pronouns   page 7
1. which — INT
2. who — REL
3. himself — RFX
4. himself — RFX
5. that — REL
6. That — DEM

Indefinite and Reciprocal Pronouns   page 8
1. one
2. all
3. each other
4. Both
5. one another
6. anything, anyone
7. everybody, everything
8. anything

Pronouns in Action!   page 9
1. Everybody, them
2. he
3. you
4. himself
5. One
6. which

Descriptive Adjectives   page 10
1. red—what color?
2. famous—what kind?
3. war—what kind?
4. young—what kind?
5. realistic—what kind?
6. red—what color?
7. dark—what kind?
8. blue—what color?
9. burly—what size?
10. tremendous—what size?
11. sinister—what kind?
12. wild—what kind?

Positive, Comparative, and Superlative Degrees   page 11
1. nearer — nearest
2. more monstrous — most monstrous
3. more nervous — most nervous
4. older — oldest
5. sillier — silliest
6. more frightful — most frightful
7. more rigid — most rigid
8. louder — loudest
9. happier — happiest
10. more peaceful — most peaceful

Limiting Adjectives   page 12
1. article
2. interrogative
3. possessive
4. demonstrative
5. numeral
6. demonstrative
7. numeral
8. possessive
9. article
10. interrogative

1. The, a
2. the, two, the, a
3. those
4. What, the
5. the
6. Henry's, this

Adjectives in Action!   page 13
1. limiting—numeral
2. descriptive
3. limiting—demonstrative
4. limiting—interrogative
5. descriptive
6. descriptive
7. limiting—article
8. descriptive
9. limiting—possessive
10. descriptive

Action and Linking Verbs   page 14
1. was—LINK
2. introduced—ACT
3. ran—ACT
4. halted—ACT
5. was—LINK
6. were—LINK
7. is—LINK, said—ACT
8. stood—ACT
9. hate—ACT
10. call—ACT
11. are—LINK
12. exclaimed—ACT

Verb Phrases   page 15
1. had gone
2. do come
3. could be heard
4. must have
5. may put
6. might have thought
7. would have been needed
8. had been obliged
9. would have been
10. was explaining

Principal Parts of Verbs   page 16
1. going   went   (have) gone
2. thinking   thought   (have) thought
3. seeing   saw   (have) seen
4. suffering   suffered   (have) suffered
5. remembering   remembered   (have) remembered
6. knowing   knew   (have) known
7. approving   approved   (have) approved
8. catching   caught   (have) caught
9. allowing   allowed   (have) allowed
10. looking   looked   (have) looked
11. speaking   spoke   (have) spoken
12. wanting   wanted   (have) wanted

Verb Tenses   page 17
1. tossed
2. knew
3. dare
4. will fall
5. managed
6. had rushed
7. find
8. carried
9. had come
10. has happened

Active and Passive Voice   page 18
1. L. M. Montgomery wrote *Anne of Green Gables*.
2. Marilla and Matthew Cuthbert took in Anne Shirley.
3. Anne was teased by Gilbert Blythe at school.
4. All students did not prepare equally for the exams.
5. Queen's, a well-known school for teachers, was attended by both Anne and Gilbert.
6. Anne dearly loved Green Gables.
7. Throughout the years this novel has been read by many young adults.

Verbs in Action!   page 19
Answers will vary.
1. present perfect
2. passive voice
3. present participle
4. future perfect
5. verb phrase

Adverbs As Modifiers   page 20
1. just—moved—when?
2. very—limp—to what extent?
3. immensely—liked—how?
4. carefully—had told—how?
5. Then—went—when?
6. everywhere—sniffed—where?
7. never—changed—how often?
8. sooner/later—meant—when?
9. quickly—can turn—how?
10. rather—amused—to what extent?

Positive, Comparative, and Superlative Degrees   page 21
1. more thoughtfully   most thoughtfully
2. later   latest
3. faster   fastest
4. more slowly   most slowly
5. more sorrowfully   most sorrowfully
6. more often   most often
7. more easily   most easily
8. more quietly   most quietly
9. lower   lowest
10. farther   farthest

1. more carefully
2. sooner
3. most athletically
4. hard
5. more closely

Adverbs in Action!   page 22
Answers will vary.

Identifying Prepositions   page 23
1. with
2. to
3. in
4. in
5. about
6. about
7. of
8. over
9. into
10. across
11. into

Prepositional Phrases   page 24
1. about children
2. for you
3. about you
4. about children
5. in spite of herself
6. on the moor
7. of earth
8. at her
9. over his eyes
10. about gardens
11. about them
12. in India
13. in the sand
14. in them
15. of earth
16. to himself
17. of something
18. to her

Adjective and Adverb Prepositional Phrases   page 25
1. of light—glimmer—adjective; beneath the door—coming—adverb
2. in that room—was crying—adverb
3. to the door—walked—adverb; in the room—was standing—adverb
4. on the bed—was lying—adverb
5. of ivory—color—adjective
6. of hair—lots—adjective; over his forehead tumbled—adverb; in heavy locks—tumbled—adverb

Prepositions in Action!   page 26
1. beside
2. to
3. of
4. like
5. on
6. below
7. in
8. down
9. with
10. instead of
11. of
12. of
13. among
14. for
15. of

Coordinating, Correlative, and Subordinating Conjunctions   page 27
1. but—coordinating
2. or—coordinating
3. both . . . and—correlative
4. and—coordinating
5. Neither . . . nor—correlative
6. Although—subordinating
7. because—subordinating
8. not only . . . but also—correlative
9. since—subordinating
10. yet—coordinating

Interjections   page 28
(Interjections will vary.)
1. !
2. ,
3. ,
4. !
5. !
6. ,
7. , or !
8. ,
9. !
10. ,
11. ,
12. ,

Conjunctions and Interjections in Action!   page 29
1. A
2. D, Indeed,
3. C
4. D, No,
5. E, No!
6. A
7. B
8. A
9. D or E, Well, or !
10. C

Kinds of Sentences   page 30
1. INT ?
2. DEC
3. EXC !
4. INT ?
5. IMP
6. EXC
7. DEC
8. IMP

Complete Subjects and Predicates   page 31
1. <u>Those tournaments</u> (are the PGA. The Masters. the U.S. Open and the British Open).
2. <u>Hundreds of golfers</u> (try each year to qualify for the professional tour).
3. <u>Qualifying tournaments</u> (are held throughout the nation).
4. <u>Several other tour events</u> (pay more money in prizes than the majors).
5. <u>The Masters' invitation list</u> (always includes the winner of the U.S. Amateur).
6. <u>A professional golfer</u> (may win money).
7. <u>An amateur</u> (cannot receive money as a prize).

8. One of the better more recent amateurs (is Tiger Woods).
9. This young sensation (won the U.S. Amateur in 1994 and 1995).
10. (Do) you (know his real name)?
11. His given name (is Eldrick Woods).
12. His nickname Tiger (has nearly replaced his real name).
13. Tiger's father (started him golfing at an extremely young age).

Simple Subjects and Verbs page 32
1. agreement (established)
2. (Do) you (know)
3. championship (was named)
4. Green Bay Packers (won)
5. They (beat)
6. Miami Dolphins (were)
7. They (beat)
8. they (became)
9. Super Bowls (have been)
10. (Will) you (watch)

Compound Subjects and Compound Verbs page 33
1. rules regulations
2. point side-out
3. (may touch) (be touched)
4. (entertains) (excites)
5. Jenni Rosa Veronica
6. (bump) (set) (spike)
7. Jenni coach
8. (will shower) (go) (rest)
9. (watched) (learned)
10. Veronica Rosa (serve) (set)

Direct Objects and Indirect Objects page 34
1. (James A. Naismith) job
2. game
3. (instructor) invention
4. contact
5. ball
6. goal
7. contact
8. (basketball) start
9. goal
10. players fans

Predicate Nouns and Predicate Adjectives page 35
1. one
2. point
3. male
4. (popular)
5. equivalent
6. (exhausting)
7. (tired)
8. (accurate)
9. (aggressive)
10. victim

Sentences in Action! page 36
Answers will vary.

Independent and Dependent Clauses page 37
1. DC
2. IC
3. DC
4. IC
5. DC

1. The four sisters sat knitting away in the twilight (while the December snow fell quietly).
2. Beth looked at her rough hands with a sigh (that anyone could hear).
3. (Although we have to work,) we make fun for ourselves.
4. I like your nice manners and refined ways of speaking (when you don't try to be elegant.)
5. (If Jo is a tomboy,) what am I please?

Simple and Compound Sentences page 38
1. SIMP
2. COMP, and
3. COMP, but
4. COMP, and
5. SIMP
6. COMP;
7. SIMP
8. COMP, and
9. SIMP
10. COMP, and

Complex Sentences page 39
1. who had pickled limes in her desk—ADJ
2. who was found breaking the law—ADJ
3. which made Jenny skip to her seat with unusual rapidity—ADJ
4. because the limes weighed upon her conscience—ADV
5. Since Amy had many—ADV
6. when the perfume met his nose—ADV
7. Because they were so disgusting—ADV
8. which created quite a little gust—ADJ
9. who were sworn foes of the girls—ADJ
10. After Amy disposed of the treat—ADV

Clauses in Action! page 40
1. Jo's face was very sober, but her eyes twinkled.
2. "Shut your eyes and hold out your arms," she said invitingly.
3. Laurie backed into a corner and put his hands behind him with a gesture.
4. Laurie heroically shut his eyes while something was put into his arms.
5. Jo, Amy, and John laughed at Laurie.
6. When John rescued his babies, Laurie laughed saying, "Twins, by Jupiter!"

Subject-Verb Agreement (Nouns) page 41
1. Appalachian Trail winds
2. It runs
3. Berkshire Hills are
4. lovers attend
5. Boston lies
6. lines mark
7. Tourists walk
8. statue stands
9. teams make
10. Harvard is

Subject-Verb Agreement (Pronouns) page 42
1. Everybody likes
2. Many travel
3. Neither knows
4. Some want
5. Several were
6. any Have
7. Everyone agrees
8. Many want
9. Most enjoy
10. All was

Subject-Verb Agreement (Compound Subjects) page 43
1. are
2. are
3. are
4. is
5. is
6. are
7. are
8. is
9. are
10. is
1. like
2. are
3. knows
4. want
5. help

Negatives page 44
1. Richard can't wait. Richard can hardly wait.
2. He hadn't gone anywhere since the trip to the Southwest. He went nowhere since the trip to the Southwest.
3. Jacob has found no postcards. Jacob hasn't found any postcards.
4. No, Susan did not see anybody. No, Susan saw nobody.
5. During the 1930s nobody did anything to prevent damage caused by strip mining in the Southwest. During the 1930s people did nothing to prevent damage caused by strip mining in the Southwest.

Frequently Confused Words page 45
1. Fewer
2. Besides
3. less
4. good
5. well
6. beside
7. then
8. than
9. good
10. fewer

Usage in Action! page 46
Answers will vary.

Capitalization (I, Days, Months, Holidays) page 47
1. B
2. B
3. B
4. A
5. B

Capitalization (Historic Events, Periods of Time, and Documents) page 48
1. Mayflower Compact
2. Articles Confederation
3. French Indian War
4. Gettysburg Address
5. Declaration Independence
6. Great Depression
7. Valentine's Day Massacre
8. Missouri Compromise
9. Emancipation Proclamation
10. Renaissance

1. Middle Ages, middle class
2. writers, Renaissance
3. Bill
4. Battle Gettysburg, battle, Civil

5. Purchase
6. industry, Industrial Revolution
7. Great Depression
8. President Bush, Desert Shield, Desert Storm

Capitalization (Names and Titles of People, Family Relationships)
page 49
1. N
2. Y
3. N
4. Y
5. Y
6. Y
7. N
8. N

1. *Wizard*
2. Uncle, Aunt
3. aunt, uncle
4. aunt, Aunt
5. L. Clemens, Mark Twain
6. uncle's, Grandfather

Capitalization (First Words) page 50
1. Lewis
2. That
3. "And
4. "'Twas, Did,
5. "Have
6. "Yes,
7. Another
8. "There
9. "Service's
10. He, "I

Capitalization (Religious Names, Races, Nationalities, Languages)
page 51
1. Y
2. Y
3. N
4. N
5. Y
6. Y
7. N
8. N
9. N
10. Y

1. Luke, John, New Testament
2. Pope, Catholic
3. Japanese, English
4. Chinese
5. Almighty

Capitalization (Geographical Names and Structures) page 52
1. east, White House
2. Chicago, Sears Tower, city
3. Lake Shore Drive, Water Tower Place, Avenue
4. North, Southeast
5. Mount Rushmore, Black, of, South
6. America, northern, Texas
7. of the, northwest
8. Leaning Tower, Italy, Tower, structures
9. Crater of, Monument, Idaho
10. Lake, Lake, Lake, Lake Erie, Lake Ontario, Lakes

Capitalization (Titles) page 53
1. St., *Dispatch*, St., *Post*, *New York World*, *Evening World*
2. *Struggling Upward*, *Ragged*
3. *San*, *News*, *Life*
4. *The Grapes*, *Wrath*
5. *Western Union*
6. *The Adventures*, *Huckleberry Finn*
7. Will Come Soft
8. *Romeo*, *Juliet*, *The Taming*, *Shrew*
9. "The Raven," "Annabel Lee," "The Tell-Tale Heart"
10. "To Build, Fire," *Youth's Companion*

Capitalization (Businesses, Organizations, Brand Names, Vehicles) page 54
1. A
2. A
3. A
4. A

Capitalization (Abbreviations, Acronyms, School Courses)
page 55
1. P.M.
2. Spanish II
3. B.C.
4. Archery 110
5. UNICEF
6. A.D.
7. CA
8. YMCA
9. FAX
10. A.M.
11. DOS
12. B.C. to A.D. 1000
13. NATO
14. NAACP

Capitalization in Action! page 56
Answers will vary.